Especially for

Mark Alan John Rascher

From

Mom & Patrick

Date

March 9/2014

© 2010 by Barbour Publishing, Inc.

ISBN 978-1-60260-807-8

Published by Barbour Publishing, Inc., P.O. Box 719, Uhrichsville, Ohio 44683, www.barbourbooks.com

Our mission is to publish and distribute inspirational products offering exceptional value and biblical encouragement to the masses.

 Member of the
Evangelical Christian
Publishers Association

Printed in China.

Fun Facts
from the
Great Outdoors

BARBOUR
PUBLISHING

In the beginning, God created the heavens and the earth.

GENESIS 1:1

Fish have six senses. In addition to the five senses that humans have, fish have a motion detection system, referred to as their "lateral line," that is made up of thousands of small hair cells. It allows them to detect the direction of vibrations, and it keeps them from bumping into each other.

Contrary to popular belief, raindrops are not shaped like we typically believe tears are shaped. Small raindrops are spherical. Larger raindrops look like a hamburger bun. And the biggest raindrops look like a parachute.

According to the U.S. Fish and Wildlife Service, sea otters have the densest, warmest fur on earth. One square inch of their fur contains as many as one million hairs—the approximate number of hairs on the heads of ten humans.

Many people are attracted to ladybugs
because of their coloring.
Ironically, their spots and colors are meant to
make them unappealing to predators.

Some people, in order to discover
God, read books. But there is a great book:
the very appearance of created things.
Look above you! Look below you!
Read it.

St. Augustine

Kansas has the largest population
of wild grouse (more commonly known
as prairie chicken) in North America.

You probably already know that all spiders have eight legs, but did you know that most spiders have six to eight eyes?

Eastport, a small port city in Maine, located on Moose Island, is the most eastern city in the United States—making it the first city in the country that sees the sunrise each morning.

Coyotes are new to Newfoundland, Canada. In 1985 the Gulf of St. Lawrence had enough ice on it to allow coyotes to enter the province from Nova Scotia.

I lift up my eyes to the hills.
From where does my help come?
My help comes from the Lord,
who made heaven and earth.

Psalm 121:1–2

Only male crickets can chirp.
The most common reason for doing so is to attract female crickets. So the next time you are sitting out on your front porch swing listening to the crickets chirp, love really is in the air.

Old Faithful, the famous geyser in
Yellowstone National Park,
erupts twenty-one to twenty-three
times each day, reaching as high as 180 feet.

Ants can carry twenty
times their own weight.

Hikers can explore more than 133,000 miles' worth of trails in America's national forests.

The best remedy for those who are afraid,
lonely, or unhappy is to go outside,
somewhere where they can be quiet,
alone with the heavens, nature, and God.
Because only then does one feel that
all is as it should be.

ANNE FRANK

According to the U.S. Fish and Wildlife Service, "Nearly three hundred species of mussels inhabit freshwater rivers and lakes in North America. This is the richest diversity of mussels found in the world."

Dragonflies have nearly 360-degree vision, which, as you might imagine, makes it easy for them to capture their prey. The green darner can fly at speeds of over fifty mph.

Pileated woodpeckers are the largest common woodpecker found in North America. They are about the size of a crow and dig such large, rectangular holes in trees in search of carpenter ants (their favorite meal) that smaller trees sometimes break in half.

Speckled garden snails are the fastest type of snail. They can move up to fifty-five yards per hour. Most other land snails can move only twenty-three inches per hour.

Sea dragons, sea horses, and pipefish are the only known species in which the male carries the eggs. Several male sea dragons have become "pregnant" while in captivity in the United States—including one in Georgia.

Every state except Alaska, Hawaii, and Maine is known to be home to at least one poisonous snake species.

The Coachella Valley fringe-toed lizard is a species unique to the Coachella Valley Wildlife Refuge in California. It is currently considered an endangered species.

Carolina wrens, found mostly in the
southern states—although some venture
as far north as the Great Lakes—
are monogamous, and pairs usually
stay together for years.

During the winter, North American river otters use ice holes in the surface of the water to breathe, and they can hold their breath under water for as long as eight minutes.

When I look at your heavens, the work
of your fingers, the moon and the stars, which you
have set in place, what is man that you are mindful
of him, and the son of man that you care for him?

PSALM 8:3–4

Nature is the art of God.

Dante Alighieri

More than 10 percent of all animal and plant species make their home in the United States, and thousands of these native species live nowhere else on earth.

According to the United States Geological Survey, approximately fifty volcanoes erupt each year in the United States; however, most are not severe. The U.S. ranks third (behind Indonesia and Japan) in the world in the number of historically active volcanoes.

The U.S. Fish and Wildlife Department says that bears don't truly hibernate because their sleep is not deep and their body temperatures fall only a few degrees below normal. But they do sleep away the harshest part of the winter.

The highest point in Pennsylvania is lower than the lowest point in Colorado.

In 1887 Montana ranch owner Matt Coleman reported the largest snowflake ever recorded. It was fifteen inches wide and eight inches thick.

Prairie plants have deep roots and are designed to survive fires. In fact, according to the National Park Service, "Prairies need disturbances such as drought, fire, and grazing to survive."

The largest brown bears in the world are found in British Columbia and Alaska, and on islands such as Kodiak. The average brown bear weighs seven hundred pounds.

According to The Nature Conservancy,
the bison is the largest land animal in
North America, with adult males standing
some six feet tall at the shoulder
and weighing up to a ton.

The Wrangell-St. Elias National Park and Preserve is the largest national park in North America, spanning 13.2 million acres, including an active volcano, many large glaciers, and nine of the sixteen tallest mountain peaks on the continent.

Death Valley is the hottest, driest, and lowest place in the United States. Temperatures often reach 120 degrees during the summer. The lowest point is 282 feet below sea level. Death Valley averages less than two inches of rain per year.

God writes the gospel not in
the Bible alone, but on trees and
flowers and clouds and stars.

MARTIN LUTHER

The Mammoth-Flint cave system in Kentucky is the largest underground cave in the world. Estimates about the length of the mapped cave system range from 300 to 350 miles.

Every year, between November and February, more than five hundred bald eagles winter in the Klamath Basin National Wildlife Refuge, located in Northern California. It's the largest gathering of bald eagles in the continental United States.

The heavens declare the glory of God,
and the sky above proclaims his handiwork.

PSALM 19:1

Blizzards in Antarctica produce winds of up to 199 mph—the strongest winds on the planet.

In 1947 the coldest temperature recorded in North America occurred at the Snag Airport in Canada's Yukon Territory: eighty-one degrees below zero.

National forests in America encompass
more than 190 million acres of land—
an area nearly the size of Texas.

In 2006 a 176-year-old tortoise named
Harriet died in an Australian zoo.
She was believed to be one of the
world's oldest living creatures.

The Lost Sea in Craighead Caverns in Sweetwater, Tennessee, is the world's largest underground lake. It covers 4.5 acres and can be found 140 feet below the surface.

Lightning can reach more than five miles. It can also raise the temperature of the air as much as fifty thousand degrees, and it contains one hundred million electrical volts.

The city of Tonopah in Nevada, located halfway between Las Vegas and Reno, was named one of the best stargazing destinations in the United States by *USA Today*. According to the Nevada Commission on Tourism, seven thousand stars can be seen from Tonopah on clear, moonless nights.

Walk away quietly in any direction and taste the freedom of the mountaineer. Camp out among the grasses and gentians of glacial meadows, in craggy garden nooks full of nature's darlings. Climb the mountains and get their good tidings.

John Muir

The Sawtooth National Recreation Area,
just north of Sun Valley, Idaho, is the
largest recreation area in the United States.
It covers 756,000 acres and contains more than
three hundred lakes and six mountain ranges.
And the public can fish, hike, ride horses,
go whitewater rafting,
and enjoy many other activities.

The official state motto for Minnesota is "The Land of 10,000 Lakes." According to the Minnesota Department of Natural Resources, Minnesota has 11,842 lakes that cover at least ten acres each.

Pisgah National Forest, located just north of Brevard, North Carolina, is home to a sixty-foot natural slide called Sliding Rock. It's a gently sloping waterslide down which eleven thousand gallons of water per minute flow. Those who use the slide end up in a six-foot-deep pool at the bottom.

On March 29, 1848, an enormous ice dam formed and stopped the flow of water over Niagara Falls for thirty hours. Eventually the water broke through and resumed its flow.

The Montana Dinosaur Trail is made of up fifteen stops throughout the state and contains unique paleontology displays, skeletal replicas, and actual skeletons of dinosaurs and other fossils found in Montana.

The Alabama Scenic River Trail is the longest water trail in the country. It is 631 miles long and winds around nine lakes, seven rivers, and two creeks.

Even the sparrow finds a home,
and the swallow a nest for herself,
where she may lay her young, at your altars,
O Lord of hosts, my King and my God.

Psalm 84:3

Kobuk Valley National Park isn't your run-of-the-mill national park. It has no roads, gift shops, trails, campgrounds, or parking. To access the beautiful 1.7 million acres, a plane ride is necessary.

Even though Mount St. Helens in Washington remains an active volcano, climbers are allowed on the mountain. If they intend to climb above 4,800 feet, they must have a climbing permit. And, of course, climbers are warned that volcanic hazards may occur without warning.

Name _____

Address _____

_____Prov_____

PC_____ Tel ( ) _____

e-mail _____

❑ Please send free catalogue and details of mail-order
❑ Please send details on Representatives & Distributors
❑ Please e-mail info regularly about new products

Book title _____

Bought at _____

Comments _____

_____

_____

_____

TRUDEN BOOKS
DENNIS and TRUDY RAMSAY
1462 - 105th St.
North Battleford, SK S9A 1T3
Phone 445-6857

THANK-YOU FOR BUYING THIS BOOK
You may use this card as a book-mark, or use it as a post-card and mail it to us with your comments. When you do, we'll send you our free colour catalogue, with no obligation!

LIVING BOOKS is a company dedicated to making a positive impact on Canada through the distribution of inspirational books.

We do this by placing Family Reading Centres in stores across Canada. We also supply and support independent Representatives and Distributors that...

- have Home Exhibits with friends & family
- place books in schools, camps, churches, etc.
- service book racks in area stores
- recruit and disciple a team of sellers

DO YOU WANT TO GET INVOLVED?
Please call or mail this card today!

www.LivingBooks.ca

BUILDING STRONG FAMILIES BY SELLING GOOD BOOKS

The Grand Canyon is 277 river miles long,
up to 18 miles wide, and a mile deep.

We can learn a lot from trees:
they're always grounded but never
stop reaching heavenward.

EVERETT MÁMOR

According to PBS, "Flamingos are some of the only creatures designed to survive in the caustic environment of a volcanic lake." They have a filter-feeding system that allows them to filter as many as twenty beakfuls of water per second.

Lake Superior is the world's
largest freshwater lake.

The first known nearly complete skeleton
of a dinosaur was found in Haddonfield,
New Jersey, in 1858.

According to PBS, "American alligators live only in fresh water in rivers, marshes, and lakes in the southeastern part of the U.S. American crocodiles like brackish or salt water and are found only in the southern tip of Florida. Crocodiles are very sensitive to the cold and stay where it's warmest."

In 1992 the late Howard "Rip" Collins caught a forty-pound four-ounce brown trout in the Little Red River (Arkansas), setting a new world record that still stands.

All spiders have and use venom to kill their prey, but not all spiders have the ability to bite humans. Exceptions include black widows and brown recluse spiders.

Missouri is known as the Show Me State,
but it is also known as the Cave State.
It has more than 6,200 caves.

Ever wonder what beavers eat?
They eat a layer of wood called the cambium
that is located just under the bark of trees.
They favor beech, maple, willow, birch, alder,
and aspen trees. They are also fond of
aquatic vegetation, buds, and roots.

To me a lush carpet of pine needles or spongy grass is more welcome than the most luxurious Persian rug.

HELEN KELLER

North America is home to
19 out of 150 owl species.

Who has ascended to heaven and come down?
Who has gathered the wind in his fists?
Who has wrapped up the waters in a garment?
Who has established all the ends of the earth?
What is his name, and what is his son's name?
Surely you know!

Proverbs 30:4

In 1872 President Ulysses S. Grant signed a bill creating the world's first national park, Yellowstone, as a "pleasuring-ground for the benefit and enjoyment of the people."

The Dungeness National Wildlife Refuge in Washington state houses the longest natural sand spit (a buildup of sand that projects into a body of water) in the United States. It is called the Dungeness Spit and is 5.5 miles long.

According to the Arkansas Department of Parks and Tourism, "The depth of Blue Spring near Eureka Springs has never been determined. It has been scientifically probed to 510 feet, and legends say an anvil was once lowered into the spring on 900 feet of rope without touching the bottom."

Canada has a longer coastline than
any other country in the world.
It is 56,453 miles long.

More than fifty million bison used to roam the Great Plains and much of North America. Most of them were killed by settlers in the nineteenth century for food and other reasons, and they were eventually reduced to just a few hundred. But they've made a comeback. Approximately 200,000 are in existence today.

Mount Everest is often referred to as the tallest mountain in the world at just slightly more than 29,000 feet. But an inactive volcano on the island of Hawaii called Mauna Kea is taller at 33,465 feet, but most of it is under water—only 13,796 feet stand above sea level.

Carlsbad Caverns National Park in New Mexico contains 113 underground caves that formed when sulfuric acid dissolved limestone and created what are known as some of the largest caves in North America.

Rainbow Bridge, a National Monument located on the edge of Lake Powell in Utah, is the largest natural bridge in the world—standing at 290 feet tall and 270 feet across. Shaped like a rainbow, it is higher than the nation's capitol building and nearly as long as a football field.

The highest tides in the world can be found in the Bay of Fundy, which separates New Brunswick from Nova Scotia. The difference between high tide and low tide there is fifty-three feet, six inches—which is about as tall as a three-story building.

Climb up on some hill at sunrise.
Everybody needs perspective once
in a while, and you'll find it there.

ROBB SAGENDORPH

The largest white sturgeon ever caught
was hauled out of the Snake River in Idaho in 1898.
It weighted fifteen hundred pounds.

The last river to be discovered in the continental United States was the Escalante River in Utah. It was discovered in 1872.

The Mississippi River is the largest river in North America. If you measure the river system from the headwaters of the Missouri River to the Gulf of Mexico, it is 3,710 miles long.

Weeping Water, a small town in Nebraska, contains the largest limestone deposit in the United States.

For thus says the LORD, who created
the heavens (he is God!), who formed
the earth and made it (he established it;
he did not create it empty, he formed it
to be inhabited!): "I am the LORD,
and there is no other."

ISAIAH 45:18

Seventy-five percent of the total land in West Virginia is occupied by forests.

Nebraska has more miles of rivers than any other state in the United States.

The largest sycamore tree in the world is located in Webster Springs, West Virginia.

Fairmount Park (9,200 acres)
in Philadelphia is nearly eleven
times bigger than Central Park in
New York City (843 acres).

The Great Salt Lake in Utah covers more than one million acres. It is seventy-five miles long and thirty-five miles wide.

To sit in the shade on a fine day,
and look upon verdure, is the
most perfect refreshment.

JANE AUSTEN

Breaux Bridge, Louisiana, is the crawfish capital of the world. Birchwood, Wisconsin, is the bluegill capital of the world. Fort Thompson, South Dakota, is the paddlefish capital of the world. Waterville, Minnesota, is the bullhead capital of the world. And Okeechobee, Florida, is the speckled perch capital of the world.

Hells Canyon, located between Idaho and Oregon, is eight thousand feet deep. It is the deepest river gorge in North America.

Michigan has more than one hundred species of trees, which makes it a beautiful place to visit as the leaves begin to change color in mid- to late-September and into October.

National Hunting and Fishing Day
is celebrated on the fourth
Saturday of every September.

The most isolated population on earth is Hawaii. It is more than twenty-three hundred miles from California, nearly four thousand miles from Japan, and almost five thousand miles from China.

The Tennessee Aquarium in Chattanooga is the largest freshwater aquarium in the world.

The Canada (not "Canadian") goose can be found in all forty-eight states in the continental United States and every province in Canada. They live twenty-four years on average and migrate to the southern portions of the U.S. and Mexico.

I love to think of nature as an
unlimited broadcasting station through which God
speaks to us every hour, if we will only tune in.

George Washington Carver

Let heaven and earth praise him,
the seas and everything that moves in them.

PSALM 69:34

"Bridge Day," an annual celebration of the New River Gorge Bridge near Fayetteville, West Virginia, occurs on the third Saturday of October—featuring parachuting and bungee jumping rom the 876-foot-tall span.

Migratory birds that are looking for a break often stop at the Clive Runnells Family Mad Island Marsh Preserve, located on the Texas Gulf Coast between Louisiana and Mexico. As many as 250 different species visit there.

In 2001 the U.S. Forest Service adopted the "Roadless Areas Conservation Rule." About one-third of the national forest system's total acreage is now off-limits to road building, which will protect more than sixteen hundred threatened, endangered, or sensitive plant and animal species.

Minnesota has twenty-six designated canoeing routes consisting of 3,353 miles.

The EPA says that wetlands in the United States fall into four general categories—marshes, swamps, bogs, and fens.

One-tenth of the forests in the world can be found in Canada.

Even if I knew that tomorrow
the world would go to pieces,
I would still plant my apple tree.

MARTIN LUTHER

Some sharks have babies by laying egg cases,
and some sharks give birth to live pups.
Either way, once they are born,
baby sharks are on their own.
They don't receive any parental care.

Porcupines have as many as thirty thousand quills that measure three inches in length.

Santa Fe is the highest capital city in the United States. It is seven thousand feet above sea level.

The Venus flytrap is native to Hampstead, North Carolina.

The Butterfly House at the Huntsville Botanical Garden in Alabama contains the largest open-air butterfly house in the United States.

Metairie, Louisiana, is the home of the longest bridge over water in the world. The Lake Pontchartrain Causeway is twenty-four miles long and connects Metairie with St. Tammany Parish.

In a tradition that dates back to the time of President Harry Truman, the current president of the United States pardons at least one turkey every Thanksgiving. Sometimes the turkey is used in Thanksgiving Day parades, and sometimes it is given to a zoo.

Sing to him; sing praises to him;
tell of all his wondrous works!

1 CHRONICLES 16:9

God Almighty first planted a garden.

FRANCIS BACON

In 1934 the fastest wind speed ever recorded in the United States was recorded on top of Mt. Washington in New Hampshire. The wind reached 231 mph.

California grows more than 300,000 tons of grapes annually.

Montana offers 3,700 miles of groomed trails for snowmobilers.

The Mackenzie River—which begins at the Great Slave Lake in the Northwest Territories and flows north into the Arctic Ocean—is the longest river in Canada. It is approximately 671 miles long, and if you include the entire Mackenzie River system, it extends more than 2,600 miles.

Manitoba has 100,000 glacial lakes in which eighty different species of fish exist.

The San Andreas Fault in California
moves about four-tenths of an inch each year.

In 1950 a bear cub was trapped in a tree during a fire in the Lincoln National Forest (New Mexico). He survived and ended up becoming the basis for the beloved "Smokey the Bear" cartoon character who encouraged people to help prevent forest fires.

If you take a canoe trip in the Mississippi River Gorge, located between Minneapolis and St. Paul, you may think you are nowhere close to civilization, but you will really be in the center of a large metropolis.

If the sight of the blue skies fills you with joy,
if a blade of grass springing up in the fields has
power to move you, if the simple things of nature
have a message that you understand, rejoice,
for your soul is alive.

ELEONORA DUSE

North America's highest peak,
Mount McKinley (Denali) in Alaska,
stretches 20,320 feet into the sky.

The Appalachian National Scenic Trail, visited by an estimated four million people annually, stretches nearly 2,200 miles from Maine to Georgia.

The Emmons Glacier, located on the northeast side of Mount Rainier in Washington, is the largest glacier in the forty-eight contiguous states. It consists of 4.3 square miles.

According to New York's Erie County Web site, "Lake Erie is the shallowest, warmest, most southern and most biologically productive of all the Great Lakes."

Praise the LORD from the earth,
you great sea creatures and all deeps,
fire and hail, snow and mist,
stormy wind fulfilling his word!

PSALM 148:7–8

John MacGregor, an English lawyer, is believed to have been the first person to develop the idea of modern sport canoeing. He took long canoe trips throughout Europe and wrote several books between 1849 and 1869 about his adventures.

According to the Yahoo! Education Web site, "The first significant achievements in mountain climbing were the ascents of Mont Blanc made by Jacques Balmat and Michel G. Paccard (1786) and by Horace B. de Saussure (1787)."

Ever wonder what the fastest-eating mammal is? The answer is the star-nosed mole. Dr. Kenneth Catania at Vanderbilt University recorded the average "handling time" as 230 milliseconds. The fastest time was 120 milliseconds.

Bayou Bartholomew is believed to be
the longest bayou in the world. It begins northwest
of Pine Bluff, Arkansas, and flows approximately 359
miles through nearly one million acres of land,
then crosses into Louisiana before joining
the Ouachita River.

The Route Verte is the most extensive bicycle route in North America. Found in Quebec, it is more than 4,000 kilometers (2,485 miles) long, and it includes bikeways, bike paths, designated shared roadways, and paved shoulders.

The History Channel notes this tidbit about the state of Michigan: "Though it is the Wolverine State, it is widely believed that there are no longer any wild wolverines in Michigan."

No site in the forest is without significance, not a glade, not a thicket that does not provide analogies to the labyrinth of human thoughts. Who among those people with a cultivated spirit, or whose heart has been wounded, can walk in a forest without the forest speaking to him?

HONORÉ DE BALZAC

Orienteering started as a military exercise in Scandinavia in the late nineteenth century. Participants race cross-country as quickly as possible while navigating with a map and a compass.

Bird-watchers in Worcester County, Maryland, have reported seeing more than 350 different species of birds.

The Lewis and Clark Scenic Byway, named after explorers Meriwether Lewis and William Clark, is eighty-two miles long. It takes modern-day explorers through two national wildlife refuges in eastern Nebraska where they will see migrating snow geese, bald eagles, and many other animals.

The honey bee is the official insect for the following states: Arkansas, Georgia, Kansas, Louisiana, Maine, Mississippi, Missouri, Nebraska, New Jersey, North Carolina, Oklahoma, South Dakota, Utah, and Wisconsin.

RAGBRI (Register's Annual Great Bicycle Ride Across Iowa) is the longest, largest, and oldest touring bicycle ride in the world. The event averages 472 total miles (68 miles per day) for the seven-day event.

In 1972 the Buffalo National River, located in the heart of the Ozarks, was named as the first federally protected stream. The river is 150 miles long and eventually joins the White River.

The 225-mile-long Katy Trail State Park in Missouri advertises itself as being suitable for avid cyclists, history buffs, and nature lovers. It is built along the former corridor of the Missouri-Kansas-Texas Railroad and is covered with hard-packed gravel.

For I will pour water on the thirsty land,
and streams on the dry ground;
I will pour my Spirit upon your offspring,
and my blessing on your descendants.
They shall spring up among the grass
like willows by flowing streams.

ISAIAH 44:3–4

Lord, make us mindful of the little things
that grow and blossom in these days
to make the world beautiful for us.

W. E. B. DuBois

Many states have converted former railroad lines into hiking and biking trails. Pennsylvania has converted more than eighty former railroad lines, totaling more than eleven hundred miles. The surfaces vary, but many are covered with crushed limestone, which makes them accessible to people in wheelchairs.

According to The Nature Conservancy, "The largest temperate rain forests are found on North America's Pacific Coast and stretch from Northern California up into Canada."

Arbor Day was established in 1872 to encourage the planting of trees. The holiday is celebrated on the last Friday of every April.

DNA evidence shows that modern horses descended from at least seventy-seven species.

April is National Kite Month. Benjamin Franklin used kites to study the earth's atmosphere. His extensive meteorological work was continued for the next 150 years until the airplane was developed.

There are approximately 12.5 million hunters in the United States.

The longest rabbit ears ever measured were on a rabbit named Nipper's Geronimo owned by Waymon and Margaret Nipper of Bakersfield, California.
The ears were 31.123 inches long.

There's a debate about the shortest river in the world. Both the Roe River in Montana and the D River in Oregon have been measured at varying lengths between fifty-eight feet and two hundred feet.

The first Saturday in June is National Trails Day in the United States. The event started in 1993.

For a variety of reasons, gray wolves are now found in only a few areas in the continental United States, Alaska, Mexico, Europe, and Asia.

The biggest selling crop for
Missouri farmers is soybeans.

By faith we understand that the
universe was created by the word of God,
so that what is seen was not made
out of things that are visible.

HEBREWS 11:3

Poison dart frogs are only one inch long and weigh less than one ounce, but they carry enough poison to kill twenty thousand mice.

During the peak summer viewing season at the Sauta Cave in the Sauta Cave National Wildlife Refuge, 200,000 gray bats emerge from the cave.

It is not so much for its beauty that the forest makes a claim upon men's hearts, as for that subtle something, that quality of air, that emanation from old trees, that so wonderfully changes and renews a weary spirit.

ROBERT LOUIS STEVENSON

The rainiest place on earth is Mt. Waialeale on Kauai Island in Hawaii. It averages 476 inches of rainfall per year.

Hummingbirds beat their wings fifty-three times per second. And that hum you hear— it comes from the sound of the wings.

Monarch butterflies migrate to California and Mexico during the winter months—some of them flying as far as three thousand miles to get there. They have a short enough life span that only those born in late summer or early fall actually make the migration.

A researcher at Cornell University says that pigeons seem to have a built-in ability to detect the earth's magnetic fields, which is one of the ways they are able to figure out where they are. It's an ability that comes in handy for homing pigeons.

The Waianapanapa State Park in Hawaii has black sand beaches. A geologist says that black sand is created when molten lava flows directly into seawater and then fragments violently.

Water falls off the 176-foot drop at Niagara Falls (in Ontario) at the rate of 150,000 gallons per second.

In 1932 fisherman George Perry reeled in the world-record bass, a 22.25-pounder from Montgomery Lake, Georgia.

According to the History Channel,
"The oldest cattle ranch in the United States
was started in 1747 at Montauk
on Long Island."

The venom from the bite of a black widow spider is fifteen times stronger than that of a rattlesnake.

If you are into astronomy, you might want to head for Kitts Peak National Observatory in Sells, Arizona. That's where you'll find the world's largest solar telescope.

In wilderness I sense the miracle of life,
and behind it our scientific
accomplishments fade to trivia.

CHARLES LINDBERGH

So God created the great sea creatures and every living creature that moves, with which the waters swarm, according to their kinds, and every winged bird according to its kind. And God saw that it was good.

GENESIS 1:21

Here are two interesting facts about bullfrogs. Only male bullfrogs make that deep baritone call that we associate with bullfrogs in general. Female bullfrogs lay as many as twenty thousand eggs at a time.

North Dakota produces more sunflowers than any other state in the United States.

Genesee River in New York state
is one of the few rivers in the entire
world that flows from south to north.

Opened in 1922, the Hollywood Bowl
in California is the largest natural
amphitheater in the United States. It seats
close to eighteen thousand people.

There is a delight in the hardy life of the open.
There are no words that can tell the hidden spirit
of the wilderness that can reveal its mystery,
its melancholy, and its charm. The nation behaves
well if it treats the natural resources as assets
which it must turn over to the next generation.

PRESIDENT THEODORE ROOSEVELT

Pigs wallow in the mud and water to maintain a comfortable body temperature. Why? Because they don't have sweat glands.

Biologists estimate that we have yet to discover somewhere between 500 thousand and 5 million different marine species.

The farthest points in the United States are Log Point, Elliot Key, Florida; and Kure Island, Hawaii. They are 5,859 miles apart. The farthest points in the continental United States are West Quoddy Head, Maine; and Point Arena, California. They are 2,892 miles apart.

Grizzly bears weigh between three hundred and fourteen hundred pounds, and when they stand upright, they can be as tall as eight feet. During the fall, they eat as much as ninety pounds of food each day in preparation for winter sleeping habits.

Did you know that the snow goose is named such because of its white color instead of its love of snow? In fact, snow geese usually summer in the Arctic but head for the coastal United States and southward for the winter.

How wonderful, O Lord, are the works of Your hands.
. . . The beasts of the field, the birds of the air
bespeak Your wondrous will. In Your goodness
You have made us able to hear the music of the
world; a divine voice sings through all creations.

A Traditional Hebrew Prayer